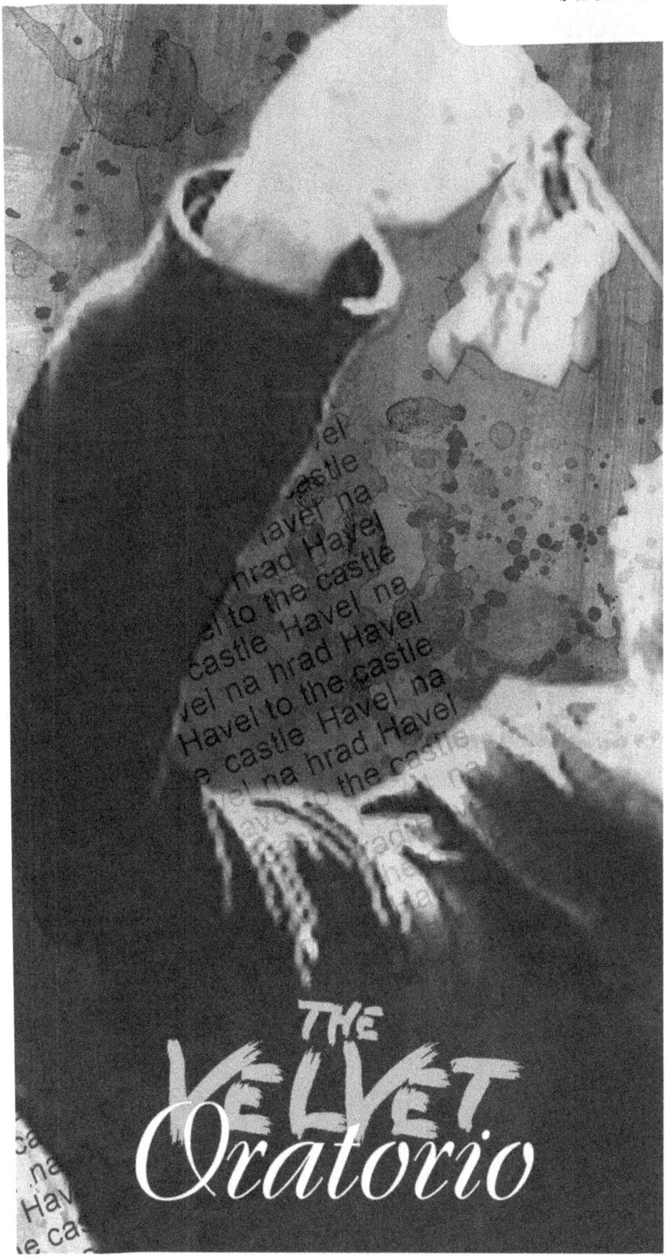
THE
VELVET
Oratorio

"Marvelous and beautifully acted"

15 MINUTES MAGAZINE

"Slyly written...often beautiful"

NEW YORK TIMES

"Sweeping. Poignant. Elegiac...Culminating in a divided society with a new playwright president leading a nation voting for the first time in nearly 50 years, The Velvet Oratorio*'s real triumph is the subtle confrontation of expectations: there is no happily-ever-after ending; if anything, the loose ends are more frayed than compounded. However, that this production can reflect the messiness of a society undergoing traumatic historic events is a testament to the scope and comprehension Einhorn and Untitled Theatre Company #61 have achieved with this delicate tribute to an era gone by."*

ART NERD

"A new music theater piece puts a human face on the Velvet Revolution in Czechoslovakia, the nonviolent people's movement that led to the fall of the Iron Curtain there in 1989...Irony, contradiction and some bawdy humor lends sympathy and humanism to the political subject"

MUSICAL AMERICA

"Incorporating primary sources, as well as scenes [based on] Václav Havel's Vánek plays ...the Oratorio *presents an impressionistic but informative overview of the heady days of the Revolution"*

JB SPINS

"A wonderfully conceived distillation in words and operatic music of what happened in Czechoslovakia after the Berlin Wall"

BLOGCRITICS

"A delicate, layered, and powerful retelling of the Velvet Revolution"

THE ARTSWIRE

Published by Theater 61 Press, a division of
Untitled Theater Company #61

Manufactured in the United States of America
ISBN 0-9770197-3-X. Second Edition

Cover and book design by Clinton Corbett.
Author photo (of Edward Einhorn) by Tanya Khordoc
Cast photos by Edward Einhorn

To the people of Czechoslovakia

Also From Theater 61 Press:

Lysistrata

The Golem, Methuselah, and Shylock

Playing Dreidel with Judah Maccabee

The Havel Collection:
The Memo
The Vanek Plays
Leaving
The Increased Difficulty of Concentration
The Pig, or Václav Havel's Hunt for a Pig

THE VELVET *Oratorio*

The Velvet Oratorio was originally presented by Untitled Theater Company #61 at the Bruno Walter Auditorium, Dorothy and Lewis B. Cullman Center, 111 Amsterdam Avenue, The New York Public Library for the Performing Arts (at Lincoln Center) on Thursday, November 19, 2009; and subsequently at the Bohemian National Hall, 321 East 73rd Street on Monday, November 30, 2009. It was created for the festival: Performing Revolution in Central and Eastern Europe, sponsored by the New York Public Library for the Performing Arts, in New York City.

2009 PRODUCTION TEAM

LIBRETTO
Edward Einhorn

MUSIC/STAGING
Henry Akona

DRAMATURGY
Karen Lee Ott

MUSICAL DIRECTOR
James Kennerley

VIDEO DESIGNER
Jared Mezzocchi

COSTUME DESIGNER
Carla Gant

ASSISTANT MANAGER
Tom Berger

STAGE MASTER/CELLO
Marissa Bea

CONCERT DIRECTOR
Michael Midlarsky

Yvonne Roen, Peter Brown, Joe Gately

2009 CAST

Civic forum. . . . . .Craig Anderson

Embassy aide. . . . . .Timothy Babcock

Communist spokesman. . . . . Danny Bowes

Vaněk. . . . . Peter Brown

Martin 1. . . . . Jonathan Farmer

Shirley Temple Black. . . . . Andrea Gallo

Michael. . . . . Joe Gately

Martin 2. Josh Hartung

Student. . . . . Uma Incrocci

Staněk. . . . . Eric Oleson

Vera. . . . . Yvonne Roen

Officer . . . . Tony Torn

Choruses sung by members of the Choir of the Church of Saint Mary the Virgin, Times Square

The 2014 - 2015 production of *The Velvet Oratorio* was presented by Untitled Theater Company #61, in association with The Consulate General of the Czech Republic in New York and The Czech Center. It was performed at the Bohemian National Hall, 321 East 73rd Street on November 8 and 9, December 12 and 13, and January 13 and 14.

2014 PRODUCTION TEAM

LIBRETTIST
Edward Einhorn

COMPOSER/ DIRECTOR
Henry Akona

SCENIC/MEDIA DESIGNER
Bryce Cutler

COSTUME DESIGNER
Carla Gant

LIGHTING DIRECTOR
Jeff Nash

MUSIC DIRECTOR
Maria Dessena

ASSISTANT DIRECTOR
Candice Dickinson

STAGE MANAGER
Andreas Hager

CONCERT MASTER
Michael Midlarsky

WARDROBE
Cristina Madero

GRAPHIC ART
Clinton Corbett

BOX OFFICE
Patrice Miller

INTERN
Jennifer Vasquez

Partial 2014 Cast

2014 CAST

Civic forum. . . . . .Craig Anderson

Officer (November shows). . . . . .Ross DeGraw

Shirley Temple Black . . . . Andrea Gallo

Baritone. . . . . John Gallop

Communist . . . . .Jonathan Kline

Student 2. . . . . .Jillian Kuhl

Martin 2 . . . . Mike Maloney

Mezzo/Soprano solo. . . . . . Jenny Lee Mitchell

Michael . . . . Mick O'Brien

Staněk . . . . Eric E. Oleson

Vera . . . . Yvonne Roen

Embassy aide . . . . .Anna Marie Sell

Student 1 . . . . Emily Shankman

Student 3 . . . . Phoebe Silva

Soprano/Mezzo solo . . . . Moira Stone

Tenor solo . . . . .Terence Stone

2014 CAST (continued)

Tenor soloist . . . . .Terence Stone

Officer (December and January) . . . . Tony Torn

Ferdinand Vaněk . . . . Matthew Trumbull

Martin 1 . . . . .Michael Villastrigo

Musicians . . . . .Oliver Fetter (Drums), Jennifer Harder (Trumpet, December and January), Marina Kifferstein (Violin), Naday Meykson (Violin), Michael Midlarsky (Cello), Nick Revel (Viola), Rebecca Steinberg (Trumpet, November)

SPECIAL THANKS TO:

Aura Pont, Laura Blum, Karen Burke, Bar 9, Stuart Burgess, William and Mary Ann Campbell, The Czech Center, Jackie Davis, Jana Dehovitz, Martin Dvořak, Sarah Engelke, Gita Fuchsova, The Reverend Stephen Gerth, Chris Harwood, Christopher Heilman, Halka Kaiserova, Selma Kalousek, Barbara Karpetova, Trey Kay, Tanya Khordoc, Jonathan Kline, Monika Koblerova, Irena Kovarova, Radka Krizek, Daniel Leventritt, Marek Milde, Pavla Niklova, Martin Palouš, Cheryl Raymond, Marcel Sauer, Obadiah Savage, Jitka Sloupova, Erin Smiley, Janet Stapleton, Sam Walters, Paul Wilson, Hana Worthen, Connie Wu, and the Untitled Theater Company #61 board

I wish to express my deep gratitude to Václav Havel, who was extraordinarily generous with Untitled Theater Company #61 throughout our time working with him, allowing us to produce his full works in our Havel Festival and to use his work (both literary and political) as an inspiration for our current piece. He is deeply missed. Truth and love must prevail over lies and hatred.

WHO AND WHERE: IN HISTORICAL PERSPECTIVE

Ladislav Adamec: The Prime Minister of Czechoslovakia during the time of the Velvet Revolution. A member of the Communist Party.
Edvard Beneš: A member of the Czechoslovak National Socialist Party, he became the 2nd President of Czechoslovakia (after Masaryk) in 1935. He opposed Germany's claim to the German-speaking Sudetenland in 1938. In October, the Sudeten Crisis brought Europe to the brink of war, which was averted only as France and Great Britain signed the Munich Agreement, which allowed for the immediate annexation and military occupation of the Sudetenland by Germany. After this event, under German pressure, Beneš was forced to resign in October 1938.
Brno: The second largest Czech city.
The Civic Forum: An organization formed November 19, 1989, in response to the November 17 march and the ensuing events. It began as an almost impromptu gathering of dissidents in the basement of the Laterna Magicka and came to represent the revolution, with Václav Havel as its leader. Although not envisioned as a political party, it later transformed into one.
Shirley Temple Black: After serving as a Nixon appointee to the United Nations, she was appointed Ambassador to Ghana, then Chief of Protocol of the United States by President Ford. The peak of Black's diplomatic career came with the appointment by President George H.W. Bush to be United States Ambassador to Czechoslovakia (August 23, 1989 – July 12, 1992) and witnessed the Velvet Revolution. She commented about her Ambassadorship, "That was the best job I ever had."

Alexander Dubček: A Slovak politician who, as leader of the Communist Party and therefore of all Czechoslovakia, tried to liberalize the Communist regime in 1968. His slogan was "socialism with a human face," and his numerous reforms led to what came to be referred to as Prague Spring. However, that period of reform ended quickly, as the Soviets invaded in August of 1968 in order to reverse them. Dubček was quickly replaced by Gustáv Husák, and didn't emerge again until the Velvet Revolution, at which time he was an early favorite to become the new President. Though it became clear the public preferred Havel for that role, Dubček was elected first speaker of the federal parliament and served until his death in 1992.

Jan Fojtik: Communist ideology chief in Czechoslovakia.
Václav Havel: Playwright, political dissident, and the former president of the Czech Republic. Deemed "subversive," his writings were banned by the Communists in the 1970s. As primary author of the freedom-claiming, repression-denouncing Charter 77, he later founded and led the Civic Forum that led the struggle to drive them from power. He was elected president of Czechoslovakia on December 28, 1989 and in 1993, president of the newly independent Czech Republic. He served two terms in that position, until February 2003. Havel died in December 2011.
Miloš Jakeš: The Communist party leader in Czechoslovakia, replacing Husák in 1987. He was forced to resign due to the events of the Velvet Revolution, and was briefly replaced by Karel Urbánek, who held the position until Havel's election.
Kosice: A Slovak city located in the Eastern part of that region.
Laterna Magicka: A theater in Prague that served as the improvised headquarters of the Civic Forum.
Tomáš Garrigue Masaryk: The first President of Czechoslovakia after the nation was formed following the collapse of the Austro-Hungarian Empire in World War I. An almost legendary figure in Czech politics, he held office until 1935.
Jan Opletal: Medical student killed in Prague on October 28,1939 by Nazi storm troopers while protesting the German occupation of Czechoslovakia. His burial became an anti-German demonstration and the anniversary of his death continues to be honored.
Plzen: A historical Czech city in western Bohemia.
People Against Violence: The Slovak counterpart to the Civic Forum.
Prague Spring: A period of reform in Czechoslovak history, spanning January 1968 to August of that same year, when Soviet forces invaded Prague and ended the reforms. The reforms were led by Alexander Dubček.
Prešov: The third-largest Slovak city.
Martin Šmid: A supposed mathematics student rumored to have been killed by the police during the November 17 march. In fact, no one was killed in the march.
Peter Uhl: A Czech dissident and journalist.
Wenceslas (Square): One of the biggest public squares in Prague, and the main gathering space during the Velvet Revolution. In some ways it is more of a long boulevard than a square. Hundreds of thousands of people gathered here during the Velvet Revolution.

CONVERSATIONS WITH THE DRAMATURG

In downtown Manhattan, dramaturg Karen Lee Ott sat down with the creators of The Velvet Oratorio *a few days prior to the first rehearsal. A close collaborator, she aimed to delve into aspects of the process of developing the piece that would interest the audience. Here are excerpts from the discussions:*

Karen Lee Ott: What came first—the music or the libretto?

Edward Einhorn (EE—librettist): The libretto. I think I was hoping, at first, that the music would come first—Henry and I have worked together before, but never on music of this kind. But in retrospect, writing the libretto first probably gave me some extra freedom with my writing that I appreciated. In the revision for 2014, Henry did write some additional music for the final chorus, and I wrote the words after. So in the end, I had a chance to do it both ways.

What inspired you to write* The Velvet Oratorio*/What is your personal connection to the history of Czechoslovakia?

EE: I curated the Havel Festival in 2006, much of which fell during the month of November. It was good timing, not only with Václav Havel's 70th birthday, but with a number of Czech historical anniversaries, from Czech National Day to the anniversary of the Velvet Revolution. Obviously, President Havel's personal connection gave these events special significance, and the highlight was when Havel, Madeleine Albright, Martin Palouš (the Czech Ambassador

Which came first—the music or the libretto?

Henry Akona (HA—composer/director): The music always comes first, at least when you're writing this sort of piece.

What inspired you to write* The Velvet Oratorio*?

HA: It was initially Edward's idea to do a piece with found text in honor of the anniversary of the Velvet Revolution when he first heard about Lincoln Center Library's festival [Performing Revolution in Central and Eastern Europe] and the project grew from there.

What is your personal connection to the history of Czechoslovakia?

HA: I did a lot of research while preparing for the play [A Butterfly on the Antenna] I directed for the Havel Festival [at The Ohio Theater, Manhattan, 2006] that Havel wrote about the period and it's a fascinating time and an inspiring story that also has connections with the present day.

What questions were you interested in exploring?

HA: I was interested in exploring the idea of the crowd and my goal was to allow the audience to become to the U.N. and another hero of the revolution), and others joined us at our party celebrating the anniversary. During the festival, Havel gave me a book of all the communications the U.S. Ambassador in Prague (Shirley Temple Black) had sent to the U.S. government. Reading through them, I had the idea of using the correspondence as the basis for a play. By coincidence, it was around then that I was invited to take part in the Performing Revolution festival, and I proposed the project in that context.

What questions were you interested in exploring?

EE: How did the revolution happen after so many years—what finally broke the dam? What did it feel like to be in the midst of it? What was the role of the people as a whole versus the role of the individual? How did the nature of the revolution relate to Czech (and Slovak) character? How did we in the United States see the revolution versus the experience of those in Czechoslovakia?

Did the questions change as you were writing?

EE: One question and its corollaries were raised, with Henry's input: What did it feel like just after the revolution was over? How had life changed or stayed the same? How did the euphoria of change play into the later realities of governance?

How did you decide which historical people to include?

EE: Shirley Temple Black was obvious, since it was her part of the crowd. And that's why it had to be a chorus—because we could have conflicting points of view expressed simultaneously. We could have people agreeing or not agreeing or even subtly disagreeing and variations and second thoughts, which, if we did with speaking and without music, would be very confusing, but with a melodic contour, a rhythmic contour, a harmonic vocabulary—all of these things can convey information at once. So the audience has to make choices about what they agree with in the crowd. The questions for me were: When does a person become a group of people? When does that group become a force with a life of its own? It's something I've never seen explored theatrically before. Of course, I've seen many pieces with choruses, but in those the chorus is a monolith, not a collection of individual stories. So that's a particularly interesting aspect of our piece.

What is it about the form of an oratorio that made it appropriate for this piece?

HA: When I first started thinking about this, it seemed clear that it was a piece of theater about a group of people and the chorus or the crowd was really the main character, and once I understood that, the form of an oratorio seemed natural because it is a form in which the chorus is the star. In other oratorios the chorus doesn't have quite the same role as it does in ours, but an oratorio is by definition for orchestra and chorus.

Is there a particular oratorio that you carry around with you

correspondence that sparked the project. She is the only fully realized historical character represented. The others who appear in found text have either only a line or two or are compressions of multiple historical figures. And of course some of the major political figures of the time: Have l, Dubček, Adamec, et al, are referred to throughout.

How do you write for an audience of both Americans and Czechs—is it fair to assume that there's quite a difference in how much these 2 groups know about the events of 1989?

EE: I deliberately mix Czechoslovak and American perspectives. The found text sections are predominantly from American sources—snatches of quotes that appeared in American newspapers, the correspondence from the U.S. Embassy, etc. These sections are meant to both fill in Americans on the details of the historical events and add some hopefully amusing commentary on the events for those more familiar with the history. There are allusions I am sure not everyone in the audience will spot—both historical and literary (ie, to the plays of Václav Havel and to the Czech poem "May," by Karel Hynek Mácha, which served as a model for the 2nd chorus).
There was a pin, a brooch, that is mentioned in one of the found text sections, which depicted crossed American and Czech flags. It was coveted during the revolution. In some ways, I see *The Velvet Oratorio* as an embodiment of that pin, and of the special close

or that you've worked on in the past?

HA: I've been performing choral music since I was 10 years, so I always have it in my ear. And I would have to say that the chorus is my favorite instrument—if a chorus can be an instrument. And I love the entire repertoire, from liturgical plainsong all the way up to the present day. I just love the sound and the flexibility of the instrument.

What musical sources inspired the writing of the music?

HA: I wasn't inspired so much by specific sources as by compositional technique; an obvious choice would have been to use Czech and Slovakian and Moravian folk songs, but I felt that there's such an established tradition of expanding upon native songs and I assumed there are others who could do that much better, so I chose some compositional techniques that help tell the story. To me, it's all about telling the story—it's not music for music's sake, it's not music to sound pretty; it doesn't exist without telling the story.

What were the greatest challenges in developing* The Velvet Oratorio*?

HA: I spent more time thinking about the form and the forces than I did writing it because there were so many choices, for example, rock 'n' roll would have been the obvious choice to capture the spirit of the time, so I considered
all rock, then an electrified string quartet or just one electric guitar fading in and out with a string quartet, but I realized rock is by

relationship our nations share. Of course, it reflects my own status as an American with a love of the Czech people.

Did you confront unanswerable historical questions during the development of the piece?

EE: When did the people realize that there was an actual revolution happening? When did they think they might actually not just reform the government, but overthrow it? When did the Communists realize it was over? Why exactly was no one killed?

These are not completely unanswerable—in fact, I try, at times, to approach answers to all of them. In other words, these are questions whose answers can never be fully known. I did a series of interviews to help research this project, and the answers I got to each question were slightly different. They were all accurate, but came from different perspectives, all valid. History almost never happens in a moment—it is a continuum, and if one person says the revolution really began when the Berlin Wall fell and another says it really started with Charter 77 (in 1977) and another says it didn't become a full revolution until the general strike on November 27—well, these are all correct. And incomplete.

***What were the greatest challenges in developing* The Velvet Oratorio?**

EE: Writing the lyrics for Henry's music. It was a form of lyric writing I had never done before, and I went through many, many drafts before I was able to discover a style that worked with the music.vz definition a very thick, broad sound with a lot of vibration, so it is not conducive to telling as many as four stories at once. So we needed something more agile, more piercing, and more controllable. Therefore, I chose a more traditional oratorio force using string quartet because it gave me the flexibility to tell the story in the most effective way. Also, I didn't want it to become precious or propaganda or pseudopatriotic, so we tried to bring in humor, contradiction, and cowardice. Not everyone is a hero; it's not a simple play nor is the music simple. If we've done our job right, the audience experiences the conflicting emotions at the end of a revolution: in this version, people go home and go to the movies.

How do you write for an audience of both Czechs and Americans?

HA: I wrote this piece for an American audience because I knew it would be in English and performed in New York. If it were ever performed before a Czech audience in Czech, I would hope they would appreciate and enjoy it, but the goal was to write for an American audience. It's not merely an historical anecdote; I wanted the audience to feel what it was like, not necessarily to participate in the Velvet Revolution—that just supplied the details—but to participate in a group event—any protest that aims to forge change, so it's a universal story. But it's not a unique story—India, South Africa, the Civil Rights Movement, among others, would have parallel arcs—this one happens

What else do you want to say about the creation and/or meaning of The Velvet Oratorio?

EE: Much of what occurs in the scenes or the choruses is based on the interviews I had with those who had been in Prague during the revolution. For example, Martin Palouš told me a story of being held by police just before the first march, and that story (somewhat transformed) became Scene One. Another person I interviewed talked about how she had forgotten her coat during the march, and I put that into the lyrics for the first chorus. Another inspiration was the absurd techniques the Communist government used to try to quell the revolution. For example, when the rumor spread that the student Martin Šmid was dead (even now it's not clear how exactly the rumor began), they put two students named Martin Šmid on television to say "I'm alive." Of course it was completely ridiculous—there could have been a third student named Martin that was dead. But it reminded me of a scene from Havel's *Largo Desolato*, and soon that scene was written.

In general, I wanted to capture not just the heroism of the revolution, but also the absurdism of it. What we idealize is just an action by a group of people with their own foibles. But I think that makes the revolution even more inspiring for me, not less.

And I do hope that, in part, *The Velvet Oratorio* serves as an inspiration. There are so many remaining totalitarian, or, to use Havel's phrase for the Communist government in Czechoslovakia, to lend itself particularly well to theatricalization.

What did it mean to perform the 20th anniversary of the Velvet Revolution in New York City in 2009?

HA: Well, it's funny because when the elections in Iran were disputed, one thing that some Iranian officials were saying is that they didn't want this to become a velvet revolution, and in the news accounts that I read, they used that specific term, meaning a peaceful nonviolent overthrow where the people just say enough is enough; we want something different. And it has become a model around the world of a certain type of revolution and I think it's what authoritarian governments fear the most because it has a moral authority that an armed resistance doesn't carry. The moral force is extraordinarily dangerous to those who want to maintain an authoritarian regime. No revolution, no election changes everything, but it's a step forward and people can embrace it for what it is. The final sentence of the piece is an upbeat, realistic expression: "We have plans.
"

End of Henry Akona interview

"post-totalitarian regimes." The resonances of the revolution are obvious at this moment in time, from the conflict in the Ukraine, to the student protests in Hong Kong, Turkey, or Venezuala, to the Arab Spring, to some of the recent disturbing political shifts in post-communist nations. Can they all use the Velvet Revolution as a blueprint? Of course not, each conflict is different. But I was moved to see a leader in Hong Kong quote Havel's "The Power of the Powerless." The ideas are still potent.

What sources did you use for the found text portions of the play?

EE: Reports from American (and a few British and Canadian) newspapers; the correspondence Shirley Temple Black sent to Washington; public documents released by the Czechoslovak government, the Civic Forum, and student groups in Prague; Václav Havel's speeches.

How closely do you echo scenes from Havel's plays in the sections that allude to them? How has working closely on Havel's plays affected your own writing/thinking?

EE: I try to parody his style and use the occasional quote for those who know his work well. These scenes take the themes and structure of his work and apply it to a new situation. For example, the Brewmaster from Audience is now a police officer, but the character is very similar. The use of repetition is very important in Havel's work, and I enjoy playing with that as well. I also use one of

Eric E. Oleson

Havel's favorite tricks: the long, self-justifying speech that leaves the character in a completely compromised moral position.

As for how his work has influenced my own writing/thinking: it's hard for me to say. Like any writer whose works I enjoy and have studied intensely, I'm sure it shows up in my work in ways I'm not ever fully conscious of. Certainly, when I began writing this I was surprised at how easily his style sprang from my subconscious. Directing his plays as well as reading them certainly enhanced that effect—when directing a play I try to understand it as well as if I had written it myself, and in some ways I think I begin to feel like I did.

Who is Vanek and what is his literary journey?

EE: Vaněk was a character Havel first created for his play *Audience* (a play I directed both in the Havel Festival and in 1993, the first New York production of Untitled Theater Company #61). Vaněk was clearly a stand-in for Havel himself—Vaněk is a dissident playwright who has been assigned by the government, as Havel was, to work in a brewery.

What makes the play remarkable is not just the character of Vaněk, however, but the compassion Havel shows in the play for the Brewmaster, who is being forced by the government to interrogate Vaněk. Havel later recorded the play with his friend Landovsky, and even though productions of Havel's plays were banned, that recording became so popular in Czechoslovakia that many could recite the play verbatim.

Yvonne Roen, Matthew Trumbull

Havel went on to write two more plays with Vaněk as the central character: *Protest* and *Unveiling.* But the character of Vaněk became so popular that many of Havel's friends began using him in their own plays. Even Tom Stoppard took up the practice recently, naming a character "Ferdinand" in his play *Rock 'n' Roll.* One of the most consistently repeated refrains in the Vaněk plays, especially *Audience,* is "Listen, Ferdinand" (a refrain I quote as well). Everyone desperately wants something from Vaněk, but perhaps the thing they want most is to be heard, acknowledged, and, in a way, absolved of their sins. Vaněk lives in a purer moral universe than anyone else, and they are afraid that he will judge them. They resent him for that, but they also accept it as his right. But in the end, Vaněk never condemns anyone. It is they who condemn themselves, they who hang themselves on their own words.

How did* The Velvet Oratorio *change between 2009 and 2014?

The production was different, as 2009 was more of a concert and 2014 was fully staged. And we had actors singing the roles who had the time to learn the material and perform it fully. And the orchestrations were fuller. In terms of the text, I added two solos to the music, so the audience could connect more to the individuals within the crowd. I added a bit of a hubbub, and with more actors performing the Found Text, I was able to expand that a bit more satisfyingly. And there were a few

Terence Stone

other small revisions, I always find a few places where I can tighten when I revisit a project.

Terence Stone

Tony Torn, Peter Brown

Andrea Gallo, Jonathan Kline

I

Found Text 1 (Berlin Wall)

STUDENT 1

Clamor in the East.

EMBASSY AIDE

For a multitude of Germans who cherish freedom, the day on which the Berlin Wall lost its purpose – November 9, 1989 – will be forever etched [into their memory.

COMMUNIST

Cheering East Germans swarmed across the Berlin Wall in a mass celebration Thursday night, hours after the communist nation`s embattled leaders announced that they would [throw open the nation`s western borders.

STUDENT 2

Strangers, friends and lovers by the score took turns hammering out a 12-inch semicircle from the reinforced concrete [that splits Berlin.

CIVIC FORUM

For the first time in 28 years, Potsdamer Platz, a square once known as the busiest on the continent, again resounded with the patter of feet [on cobblestones

Note: a convention of Caryl Churchill's, using an open bracket: [to indicate that the next line of dialogue begins early and overlaps the previous line

SHIRLEY TEMPLE

The Berlin Wall, the most potent political symbol of the postwar era, has, for all intents and purposes, fallen.

MARTIN 1

Dr. Helmut Kohl:

CIVIC FORUM

"We are and will remain one nation. Step by small step we will find our way to a common solution."

SHIRLEY TEMPLE

Soviet spokesman:

COMMUNIST

"The pulling down of the Berlin Wall, which has symbolized the division of Europe for many long years, is surely a positive and important fact. Our new policy contributes to the strengthening of mutual confidence and to the improvement of political life."

STUDENT 3

A Czech driver:

CIVIC FORUM

"There is no West Czechoslovakia, but if there was, I'd be the first to go."

SHIRLEY TEMPLE BLACK

Telegram. Prague, the U. S. Embassy. Shirley Temple Black, Ambassador. To the State Department. Confidential.

On the surface, Czechoslovakia appears the "island of stability" that many state officials portray. Rumors are intensifying, however, that the Jakeš regime has been more shaken than it is ready to admit by the events occurring in what was the staunchest ideological ally in the region, the GDR. But there is a paradox at work here. While the leadership may feel pressed to react to GDR developments, the popular Czechoslovak reaction has been different. It is our sense that the average man, distinct from dissident and intellectual circles, has become more, not less, cautious. The reaction is easier to understand if one can appreciate the deeply risk-adverse psychology of the Czech people. In the face of change, they prefer to opt for what they know.

COMMUNIST

Miloš Jakeš, the Communist Party leader in Czechoslovakia, remains firmly in control at a time when his fellow hard-liners have either stepped down voluntarily [or been forced to resign.

EMBASSY AIDE

"He will probably survive this year," a European diplomat said, "but he may not make it through the party congress next year, and he certainly won't settle in [for 5 or 10 years."

STUDENT 1

Some opponents of the Government hope to stage a protest on Friday to mark the anniversary of the death of one of the political martyrs in Czechoslovak history.

MARTIN 2

The protesters intend to commemorate the death of Jan Opletal, who was killed in 1939 by Nazi storm troopers while protesting the German occupation of Czechoslovakia.

STUDENT 3

Some youths are losing faith.

Ross DeGraw

Andrea Gallo

Tony Torn

SCENE 1 (AUDIENCE)

(An interrogation room, in a run-down police station. VANĚK is sitting in an awkward position, trying to avoid aggravating his hemorrhoids. OFFICER enters and slams down a dossier on his desk. He consults it.)

OFFICER

Mr. Vaněk?

VANĚK

Yes.

OFFICER

It's a pleasure to meet you, Mr. Vaněk.

VANĚK

Thank you.

OFFICER

I enjoyed your play, the one in the brewery—

VANĚK

You've read it?

OFFICER

I've confiscated it, more than once.

(Pause.)

Listen, Ferdinand—you're Ferdinand, aren't you?

VANĚK

Yes.

OFFICER

Listen, Ferdinand—you don't mind if I call you that?

VANĚK

Go ahead.

OFFICER

If you do, let me know.

VANĚK

I don't mind.

OFFICER

Listen, Ferdinard—I wanted to have a word with you.

VANĚK

Very well.

(Pause.)

How much longer will I be here?

OFFICER

Where?

VANĚK

Here.

OFFICER

I don't know. A few more hours. Maybe another day or so.

VANĚK

Another day?

OFFICER

Maybe a few more hours.

(Pause.)

Listen, Ferdinand—you sure you don't mind?

VANĚK

What?

OFFICER

When I call you Ferdinand?

VANĚK

No.

OFFICER

Listen, Ferdinand—what's the deal with this march?

VANĚK

What march?

OFFICER

This march. This march you're having.

VANĚK

I'm not having a march.

(Pause.)

A few more hours here?

OFFICER
Maybe a day. Not longer than that. You've been detained much longer, haven't you?

VANĚK
It's just the boredom. The hours.

OFFICER
Listen, Ferdinand—how many people will be there, do you think?

VANĚK
Where?

OFFICER
At the march. At this march of yours.

VANĚK
I'm not having a march.

OFFICER
Because I need to know how many men to assign.

VANĚK
What march?

OFFICER
For the student. That...Jan Opletal fellow.

VANĚK
Oh, that march. That's not my march.

(Pause.)

OFFICER

Listen, Ferdinard—you're a peaceful sort of fellow, right?

VANĚK

Certainly.

OFFICER

It's just that things could get out of hand.

VANĚK

Out of hand? How?

OFFICER

At this march of yours.

VANĚK

It's not my march.

(Pause.)

I have a problem with hemorrhoids.

OFFICER

Do you? My uncle had that problem, too.

VANĚK

It's acting up.

OFFICER

He used a cushion.

VANĚK
I have one of those. At home.

OFFICER
Yes. They can be very helpful.

VANĚK
So if you don't have any more questions for me...

(Pause.)

OFFICER
Listen, Ferdinand, it's just with what happened at the Wall—

VANĚK
What wall?

OFFICER
The Wall. The Berlin Wall.

VANĚK
What happened at the Berlin Wall?

OFFICER
Well, we just don't want things to get out of hand, is all.

VANĚK
What happened at the Wall?

OFFICER
Don't you know?

VANĚK
I've been in detention. What happened?

(Pause.)

OFFICER
Maybe I can find you a cushion.

VANĚK
I'd appreciate it.

OFFICER
It's just—if you could tell me how many people there will be at this march—

VANĚK
It's not my march.

OFFICER
It's to both our benefits, really. I mean, you're a peaceful sort of fellow.

VANĚK
Yes, but—

OFFICER
I just wouldn't want things to get out of hand.

VANĚK
I wasn't even planning on going.

OFFICER
Where?

VANĚK

To the march. For Jan Opletal. I wasn't planning on going.

OFFICER

No?

VANĚK

No.

(Pause.)

Look, I'd really appreciate it if I didn't have to stay here another day. My hemorrhoids —

OFFICER

Those can be painful. My uncle had them.

VANĚK

Yes. So you see.

OFFICER

If you could just tell your people, we don't want things to get out of hand, after the Berlin Wall—

VANĚK

What happened at the Berlin Wall?

OFFICER

It fell.

VANĚK

It fell? The Berlin Wall fell?

OFFICER

So you see, we don't want things to get out of hand—

VANĚK

The Berlin Wall fell?

OFFICER

Yes. Didn't you know?

VANĚK

I've been in detention.

(Pause.)

OFFICER

Listen, Ferdinand..

VANĚK

Yes?

OFFICER

Everything's all fucked up.

Chorus 1 (The March)

(Sung, like all the choruses, as a mix of full choir and solos from a quartet of central singers—soprano, mezzo, tenor, and baritone.)

CHORUS

Am I late?
Has it started?
Has it—
Where is—
You're not late it starts at four
All these people
Look there's Vilma
No that's Jana
No that's Vilma, see the hat?
All these people
All these students
Eva Hana Halka Blanka Karel Kristof
Kornrad Martin
No that's Vilma, see that hat?
That's not her hat
No it's mine she borrowed it
Where is—
Will you see a movie with me?
Now?
No, tomorrow
Do you have the notes from class?
No, I forgot them
You promised
I forgot them

When are we going?
We're not moving, we should go
Anton's coming, he's not here yet
He'll meet us there
Where?
At Wenceslas
Wenceslas not Vyšehrad?
Is that where we are going?
Am I late?
I just came from class, where were you?
Here we go.

Remember Jan Opletal!
We are known—
Remember Jan Opletal
Known throughout history—
Remember Jan Opletal
We are known throughout history—
Remember Jan Opletal!
Not to start revolutions

This is just another protest
No effect
This is our moment
After Berlin, it's our turn
No one will listen
Where are we going?
They won't let us go to Wencelas
Jan Opletal!
Wencelas
They won't let us
To Vyšehrad!
Freedom!
I forgot my jacket.

Freedom!
Opletal!
Berlin!
It's getting cold
Berlin! Berlin!
Who is that woman with my boyfriend?
Warsaw and Berlin!
My feet hurt in these shoes
Free elections!
If not now, when?
If not us, who?
It's finally here.

This is amazing, amazing
All these students
All these people.
It's too cold, I'm going home.
We can't let this end
Tell me what happens
To Wenceslas!
They won't let us
Give me a call
They can't stop us
To Wenceslas!
To Wenceslas!
To Wenceslas!
I'm going home

Where are we going?
Wencelas!
Who is leading?
Who's in front?
They won't let us—
Who is leading?

I'm in front but I'm not leading
Who's that—
They're ringing—
Keys?
They're ringing-
Keys!
Like bells
Ringing-
Ringing
Ringing
Hey!

What was that—
Look out
Who's pushing?
It's the—
Hey!
The police, they're—
We just want to go to Wenceslas
Let us—
Look out
Careful
Sorry, I was pushed
They're pushing
They mean business

After Wenceslas we will go home!
After Wenceslas we will go home!
After Wenceslas we will go home!

Look out, professor
Dinosaurs out!
Jakeš out!
He broke his arm

We want a new government!
The street is the voice of the people
Sit down

They're pushing
Don't move
Sit down

MEZZO

Who is listening?
Are they scared, like me?
I'm sacred.
Does it matter?
Do they care if I die?
Would it matter if I died?
Would they care if they killed us?
Would I give my life like Opletal?
No.
Not I.

CHORUS

Go! Down the alley
"No violence"
We can get out down the alley
Into the theater
In the basement of the theater
Will someone will let us in?
That apartment
Into that apartment
Look there's Vilma.
Look they're gone.
The streets are looking empty now.

They're gone.
There may be still some out there.
Be careful.
Maybe they're gone.
I'm going home
My boyfriend and I have plans
Tomorrow
A movie
We have plans.

II

Found Text 2 (November 18)

SHIRLEY TEMPLE BLACK

Telegram. Prague, the U.S. Embassy. Shirley Temple Black, Ambassador. To the State Department. This is an action message.

An officially sanctioned student commemoration on the evening of November 17 developed into Czechoslovakia's largest anti-regime demonstration in 20 years. The peaceful demonstration was brutally dispersed by truncheon-wielding riot police. An embassy aide witnessed:

EMBASSY AIDE

Journalists were particularly targeted. A CNN reporter was detained and his camera smashed. A BBC journalist was knocked unconscious. The police used an armored personnel carrier with a battering ram to squeeze the students together, until their only option was to flee into the surrounding shops and apartments. Within 30 minutes the street was clear.

STUDENTS

We, the university students of Czechoslovakia, protest most strongly against the brutal breaking up of the peaceful demonstration. This was not simply an attack on students, it was an attack on the children of workers and peasants. We demand an inquiry without delay. We demand the formation of a suitable parliamentary commission of inquiry with the participation of the university strike committees. We see no other way of expressing our disagreement and alarm.

EMBASSY AIDE

The Czechoslovak Communist ideology chief, Mr. Jan Fojtik:

COMMUNIST

"I'm certain we can establish a dialogue with reasonable people, but there can be no dialogue with those who set out to destroy our society. I foresee no significant changes."

STUDENT 1

A Czech driver:

CIVIC FORUM

"The thing has begun now and it cannot go back. People have lost their fear."

STUDENT 2

According to reports, one student has died of injuries.

COMMUNIST

Friends of the slain student said Martin Šmid fell to the ground after being struck several times on the head and shoulders. As Šmid lay flat, the police continued to beat him until his face was no [longer recognizable.

CIVIC FORUM & STUDENTS

"You can't kill [us all!"

EMBASSY AIDE

Youthful protestors placed candles at the spot on National Street where the 20-year-old mathematics student was beaten [to death

CIVIC FORUM & STUDENTS

"We won't let you [murder us!

STUDENT 3

The students faced down several lines of helmeted riot police to stand near a symbolic grave on the cobblestone sidewalk. A small card on the grave read: "Here died Martin Šmid."

SHIRLEY TEMPLE BLACK

It was a girl who had given word to

EMBASSY AIDE

name redacted

SHIRLEY TEMPLE BLACK

That her boyfriend, Martin Šmid, had died. The girl,

EMBASSY AIDE

name redacted

SHIRLEY TEMPLE BLACK

First informed him over the weekend of her experiences. The girl cannot be found. Dissident spokesman Petr Uhl was reportedly now backing away from the story. The rumor persists, despite official denials.

SCENE 2 (LARGO DESOLATO)

(VANĚK's home. MARTIN 1 and MARTIN 2 enter. They are holding stacks of paper.)

MARTIN 1

Good afternoon, sir.

MARTIN 2

Good afternoon.

MARTIN 1

Can we come in?

VANĚK

Yes, do.

(MARTIN 1 abruptly hands VANĚK his stack of papers and exits.)

MARTIN 2

Do you recognize us?

VANĚK

I can't place you, at the moment.

MARTIN 2

We've been in the news.

VANĚK

There's been so much in the news, recently.

(MARTIN 1 enters with a new stack of papers and hands them to VANĚK.)

MARTIN 2

I'm Martin, and he's also Martin.

(MARTIN 2 hands VANĚK his stack of papers and leaves.)

VANĚK

How do you do?

MARTIN 1

So you see.

VANĚK

Yes?

(Uncomfortable pause. MARTIN 2 enters with a new stack of papers. MARTIN 1 hands VANĚK his stack of papers and leaves.)

VANĚK

I'm sorry, but what are all these?

MARTINS 1 & 2

Papers.

VANĚK

So I see. This seems to be an essay of some sort...

MARTIN 2
Martin wrote it. For school.

VANĚK
And is this some sort of ticket stub...

MARTIN 2
Mine.

(MARTIN 1 enters with a new stack of papers. MARTIN 2 hands over his stack of papers and leaves.)

MARTIN 1
This is all I have.

VANĚK
I was hoping there was an end.

MARTIN 1
I can look for more.

VANĚK
Please, no more. What is this about?

(MARTIN 2 enters with his stack of papers. MARTINS 1 & 2 hand the papers over to VANĚK, who struggles with them. They topple. MARTINS 1 & 2 immediately begin sorting.)

MARTIN 1
Yours.

MARTIN 2
Yours.

MARTIN 1
Yours.

MARTIN 2
Yours.

VANĚK
What are these papers?

MARTIN 1
These are our lives.

MARTIN 2
From birth to death.

MARTIN 1
Well, not to death.

MARTIN 2
No, definitely not to death. Just till now.

MARTIN 1
Everything we ever wrote.

MARTIN 2
Everything that's ever been written about us.

MARTIN 1
Ever.

VANĚK
But...why?

(The MARTINS stand.)

MARTIN 2
Is it all right to smoke?

VANĚK
Yes, of course.

MARTIN 2
Actually, I don't smoke myself. I was asking for Martin here. He smokes like a chimney.

(MARTIN 1 feels for cigarettes, but can't find any. MARTIN 2 feels for cigarettes, but can't find any. They look at VANĚK. He feels for cigarettes. He can't find any. Pause. They return to sorting.)

VANĚK
I'm sorry, I still don't understand. Why are you giving these papers to me?

MARTIN 2
They prove I am Martin.

MARTIN 1
And that I am Martin.

VANĚK
Really?

MARTIN 1
Yes. Do you want to read them?

VANĚK
No need.

MARTIN 2
Just read a few. Then you'll believe us.

VANĚK
But I do believe you.

MARTIN 2
You believe us? You believe I am Martin?

MARTIN
And that I am Martin?

VANĚK
Yes. Why not?

MARTIN 1
Why not indeed?

(Pause.)

VANĚK
Is there—is there anything else?

MARTIN 2

So you'll tell them?

VANĚK

Tell them what?

MARTIN 1

That we came. That you believe us.

VANĚK

Tell who?

MARTINS 1 & 2

Havel.

MARTIN 1

And his lot.

MARTIN 2

You'll tell them?

VANĚK

I'm sorry, I don't think I quite understand.

MARTIN 1

You believe that I'm Martin?

MARTIN 2

And you believe that I'm not dead?

VANĚK

I most certainly believe that you're not dead.

(The MARTINS stand, each with his own stack.)

MARTIN 1

Do you have any rum?

VANĚK

Rum?

MARTIN 1

I don't drink myself, but Martin here drinks like a fish.

VANĚK

Look here, I'm just not sure what you want from me.

MARTIN 2

Want from you? We don't want anything from you.

MARTIN 1

You've got us all wrong.

MARTIN 2

We're not being clear.

MARTIN 1

We're just students.

MARTIN 2

We just wanted you to see us in person.

MARTIN 1

So that you can see that no one killed us.

VANĚK

Killed you? Why would someone have killed you?

MARTIN 2

At the march.

VANĚK

Are you saying that you're Martin Šmid?

MARTINS 1 & 2

Yes.

VANĚK

Which one of you is Martin Šmid?

MARTINS 1 & 2

Both of us.

MARTIN 1

And we're both alive.

MARTIN 2

As you see.

MARTIN 1

We're just students.

MARTIN 2

Go ahead, look at our papers.

VANĚK

Listen, you may both be Martin Šmid, but how do I know you are the Martin Šmid that was killed?

MARTIN 1

We can't be.

MARTIN 2

We aren't.

MARTIN 1

Because we're alive.

MARTIN 2

As you can see.

MARTIN 1

Here are our lives.

MARTIN 2

We have our proof, right here.

MARTIN 1

You can see that, can't you?

MARTIN 2

You can see that we're alive?

VANĚK

Yes.

MARTIN 1

Because we keep hearing that we're dead.

MARTIN 2

People keep calling my parents with condolences.

MARTIN 1

I have an apartment full of wreaths. They keep being delivered. I don't understand who's sending them.

MARTIN 2

A friend of mine wrote an obituary that was passed among the students.

VANĚK

You're alive. You're definitely alive.

MARTIN 1

Both of us?

VANĚK

Both of you, yes.

MARTIN 1

There. You see. I told you.

MARTIN 2

I told *you*.

MARTIN 1

Goodbye then. And thank you.

MARTIN

Yes, thank you.

(They turn to leave.)

VANĚK

Wait!

(They turn round again.)

Is there a third Martin Šmid, who is also a student?

(Pause.)

MARTIN 1

There is.

VANĚK

And is he alive?

(Long pause.)

MARTINS 1 & 2

I don't know.

Chorus 2
(The Death of Martin Šmid)

CHORUS

Late evening, seventeen November,
A time…
A haze of stars…
Surrounded by the candles' yellow light;
One, among the many, called out
Then fell.
Found after last light flickered out,
Silence and moonlight glare;
Pallid face reflecting silver in the light.
The people now were far away.
Alone he lay, this youth, this beautiful child.
The rage of a moment took away his dream.
The fight has come at last and he is fallen.

SOPRANO

Didn't know him.
Martin Smid.
A candle in my hand.
Martin Smid.
I never met him.
A bright candle in my hand.
Does it matter?
That he died?
Do they care?
That he died?
But that boy … like Opletal.
But that boy …
Like me.

CHORUS

Late evening, eighteen November,
The turtle dove calls:
"Martin! Martin! Martin!"
The spirits cry:
"From death's threshold we receive you.
Become one with us and welcome;
We will take you to your place."

The cobblestones:
"Lay upon us, we'll be thy resting place."

The gusting winds:
"We shall sing a song for you."

The waxing moon:
"I shall shroud you all in white."

The river mist:
"I shall be the veil of mourning."

Black night itself:
"I shall robe the mourners."

The morning dew:
"Mine shall be the tears."

The hills of Vyšehrad:
"We shall provide a place."

The moles underground:
"We shall dig his grave."

All creeping time:
"Over his bones I will grow a tomb."

The night-birds, flying past the moon:
"And we will enjoy a feast;

Who will be next, who will be next?
What shall be the next course for our feasting now?"

All say:
"It is ready, it is day, it is day, it is day."

Early morn, nineteen November.
There is no body, never was
No hero there to bury.
No Martin there at all.
The people cry:
"Too late, too late.
He never lived but died for us."

III

Found Text 3 (The Civic Forum)

COMMUNIST

At this point, the fact that no student named Martin Šmid was killed is almost irrelevant. The news has already had its effect.

EMBASSY AIDE

The government's case was not aided by the badly staged television appearances of students claiming to be Martin Šmid. The Czechoslovak audience, accustomed to government propaganda, mistakenly assumed the students to be frauds.

CIVIC FORUM

On November 19, at 10 pm, the Civic Forum was created to be the voice of Czechoslovak society, which has become progressively more critical of the policies of the present Czechoslovak leadership. The Civic Forum wishes to begin negotiations regarding their following urgent demand — the immediate resignation of the those responsible for the long years of devastation since 1968. [This concerns namely—

COMMUNIST

The Czechoslovak society is at the stage of critical reassessment of the experience of its political and economic development. This is a natural process. Most countries undergo it in one way or another. Regretfully, the need for constant socialist self-renewal and realistic appraisal has not always been taken for granted, particularly in situations when events intertwine in a contradictory way and require bold answers to the challenges of the time.

SHIRLEY TEMPLE BLACK

A Civic Forum contact tells us at the embassy that Prime Minister Adamec cancelled a proposed meeting with Václav Havel on November 23. Havel made no announcement of such a meeting at the day's demonstrations. Civic Forum members showed themselves [under considerable strain.

STUDENT 1

We appeal to you, workers and peasants, who with your daily work build the material basis for us students to have an education and thereby prepare for our future.

MARTIN 1

We think of workers who work in conditions that insult human dignity.

STUDENT 2

We think of the filth of corruption and of the black economy that affects everyone today. We turn to you to support our demands.

STUDENTS & MARTINS

And we appeal to you to participate in a general strike, to be held November 27, from noon to 2 pm, as an expression of your solidarity.

SHIRLEY TEMPLE BLACK

The following records a conversation overheard by an Embassy aide:

EMBASSY AIDE

The speakers were mostly older people, including a woman around 80 years old. They were discussing the events of the last few days and the past 50 years, back to the 1930's when Beneš was president. They were enjoying the chance to say these things out loud. One said:

CIVIC FORUM

Everyone has to participate in the general strike next week. That will show them.

EMBASSY AIDE

The old woman responded. "I heard that anyone who participates will lose his job." This statement was followed by a dead silence. Then the man spoke again:

CIVIC FORUM

They can't fire all of us.

EMBASSY AIDE

"I remember Beneš," replied the old woman "what a man, what a gentleman. You could run into him right here on the square and say 'Good day, Mr. President,' and he would say 'Why good day, how are you? Buying shoes?' Now, everyone goes everywhere in big cars. They have money, big places, everything." A young woman spoke:

STUDENT 3

The main thing is, there has to be a good turnout for the strike.

(STUDENTS, MARTINS, and CIVIC FORUM cheer.)

EMBASSY AIDE

The old lady continued. "When Beneš went into government, he got 10,000 a year. Now they get 2.5 million. They build themselves palaces. They have all the—" This word I did not understand, but it got a big laugh.

(STUDENTS, MARTINS, and CIVIC FORUM laugh.)

The first man spoke again:

CIVIC FORUM

If we all stop working, if the mines stop, they have to listen and the old men will have to get out.

EMBASSY AIDE

"What if we strike and nothing happens?" asked the old woman. Silence.

MARTIN 1

We strike again.

MARTIN 2

We keep on striking again and again.

(Another cheer.)

SHIRLEY TEMPLE BLACK

A final note. On the metro this morning this Embassy's spouse's housekeeper saw a young student wearing one of our U. S. Czechoslovak flag pins. Someone on the subway offered him 500 crowns (50 dollars) for it. The offer was refused. End note.

SCENE 3 (PROTEST)

(The home of STANĚK. VANĚK is standing holding a briefcase. STANĚK is looking at VANĚK with affection. VANĚK appears embarrassed.)

STANĚK

Vaněk! My old friend!

(STANĚK walks over to VANĚK, considers embracing him, but instead grabs him by the shoulders and gives him a shake.)

Did you have a hard time finding me?

VANĚK

Not really.

STANĚK

It's the bushes outside. I should have mentioned the bushes.

VANĚK

I had no problems.

STANĚK

Cognac?

VANĚK

Better not.

STANĚK

Come on, one symbolic sip.

(STANĚK grabs two glasses and pours.)

What shall we toast to?

VANĚK

To changing times?

STANĚK

To seeing each other again!

(STANĚK downs his drink. VANĚK takes a reluctant sip.)

How many years has it been?

VANĚK

Since '77?

STANĚK

You haven't changed.

VANĚK

Surely somewhat.

STANĚK

I'm no longer what I was. My hair is turning gray. Diseases...You used to call me an unrealistic optimist. You were such a pessimist...

VANĚK

I'm not a pessimist.

STANĚK

See how things have changed!

(Pause.)

So how are things going?

VANĚK

How do you mean?

STANĚK

At the Laterna Magicka. Your little group I mean. Havel, and all that lot.

VANĚK

The Civic Forum?

STANĚK

Yes, I heard you were calling yourselves that.

VANĚK

We're feeling like some real progress might be made.

STANĚK

No reason to be modest, Ferdinand, I've been following everything closely. The marches, the gatherings in the square. It's very impressive.

And the student strike. Did I hear you are talking about a general strike too?

VANĚK

Yes.

STANĚK

For factory workers and the like? Across the country?

VANĚK

We are asking that the essential workers continue to do their jobs, but yes.

STANĚK

You may be overreaching yourselves. Certainly, you have the students on your side, the artists, the intellectuals. But the general man—

VANĚK

We're feeling optimistic.

STANĚK

The general man isn't so interested in politics, I think. Doesn't want to risk a strike.

VANĚK

I suppose we'll find out.

(Pause.)

STANĚK

You know what you should do? Write something.

VANĚK

Write something?

STANĚK

You're a writer, aren't you? A lot of you are writers. You should write up a manifesto of some sort, get people to sign on to this Civic Forum of yours.

VANĚK

We've written one.

STANĚK

Have you?

VANĚK

Yes.

STANĚK

Yes. Yes, of course you would. How foolish of me to suggest it.

VANĚK

Would you like to see it?

STANĚK

You have a copy?

VANĚK

Yes.

(VANĚK opens his briefcase and takes out the manifesto. STANĚK glances at it.)

STANĚK

It's good. Very good. Excellent. Just what I had in mind. But do you mind if I offer some tips, some advice from the inside? There should be resignations, yes, that's true, that's definitely true. And these names...many of them are justified, more than justified, of course. But the head of the Communist Party? You go too far.

VANĚK

We believe his resignation is essential.

STANĚK

Well, it's your manifesto of course. At least you're not calling for my resignation! Of course, I'm probably not big enough for anyone to call for that. Little fish in a big pond.

(He laughs a bit uneasily.)

VANĚK

No, we're not calling for that.

(Pause.)

STANĚK

I suppose you were pretty surprised when I called.

VANĚK

In a way.

STANĚK

I understand you might want a little distance from me.

VANĚK

Me? No.

STANĚK

It hasn't been easy, Ferdinand, I'll tell you that. Working from the inside. Trying to do what little I can, in my own way. I know, some of your friends may think that I've been with them all along, that I've been lying to myself in some unforgiveable manner—

VANĚK

I'm not saying that.

STANĚK

I wouldn't blame you if you were, really. I understand perfectly well what leads to that sort of prejudice...

(Pause.)

I just wish there was a way for me to help.

VANĚK

There is, actually.

STANĚK

Is there?

VANĚK

Come to Wenceslas Square on Sunday. The Prime Minister will be there, too.

STANĚK

The Prime Minister?

VANĚK

And so will a lot of us who were there in '68. You were there, with us, fighting with us. Before you.... Some people remember you, from then.

STANĚK

I *was* there.

VANĚK

I will ask Havel to let you speak.

STANĚK

They will think I am opportunistic, speaking now.

VANĚK

You can tell them that your essential views never changed.

STANĚK

But what of my job?

VANĚK

This administration won't be around much longer.

STANĚK

What if it is?

(Pause.)

I could speak out now, it's true. It would lift a heavy burden off of me. I would win back my self-esteem, my freedom and my dignity, after years of struggling between my conscience and a certain sort of practicality. Of course, I will risk my job, but as you say, this administration may be on its way out anyway. Of course if it's not, the implications for me and my family would be enormous. What of that, you must say, you have risked yourself, Ferdinand, you have even gone to jail for your convictions, and meanwhile what have I done but conform. But I have a family to worry about, not just myself. If I do speak, it will matter little to anyone but me – after all, with Havel and the Prime Minister there, no one will care what I have to say, and even what they hear they will scarcely believe. There are so many more with greater credentials than me. People will accuse you of using me, of forcing me to speak and forcing me to risk my wife and children in so doing. It won't be fair to you, of course, but there it is. Don't misunderstand me, Ferdinand, I don't think so, and I wouldn't be swayed by such thinking, but in the end this is a political decision, and a good politician must weigh all factors. Under these circumstances, the question is, what should I choose: the liberating inner emotions that speaking out will bring, the chance to finally slip out of my years of bondage, or will I continue on the same conservative path that I have, refusing to risk losing what it has taken me years to build up for what is, honestly speaking, a politically insignificant act in the scheme of things, yet living still longer with the bitter realization that I have once again, and perhaps for the very last time, missed the chance to shed myself of the humiliating compromises I have made over the years?

VANĚK

It seems clear.

STANĚK

To me as well.

VANĚK

That you...

STANĚK

Unfortunately...

VANĚK

Unfortunately?

STANĚK

You thought that...?

VANĚK

My apologies. I didn't understand you.

(Pause.)

STANĚK

Are you angry?

VANĚK

No.

STANĚK

I'm no longer what I was. My hair is turning gray. Diseases...

VANĚK

I understand.

STANĚK

Good luck, with your Forum. .With your general strike. Tell them...Tell them...

VANĚK

Yes?

STANĚK

Perhaps it would be best if you didn't tell them anything at all.

Chorus 3 (The Strike)

CHORUS

November twenty-seven, Noon
In Pardubice Worker K
Along with Workers A through J
Called "Strike"
Factories are silent.
Outside it is loud.
Factories are empty.
Outside is a crowd.
Worker D cries "Freedom"
"Democracy," says Worker F
"Truth" shouts C and B yells "Justice"
D through H call "Dubček!"

November twenty-seven, Noon
In Prešov Chief Assistant L
Along with Supervisor M
Call "Strike".
Offices are silent.
Outside it is loud.
Offices are empty.
Outside is a crowd.
Supervisor and Assistant
Both chant out in concert
"Czech and Slovak must be good,
Havel is our Robin Hood."

Inside it is dying.
Inside rooms of power where our leaders sit and rule.
Inside where they're hiding.
Building walls of paper.

Inside their brown buildings.
Brown suits covering brown souls.
They shuffle and they whisper.
Is it over?
What will they do now? If it's over?
They write up proclamations, propaganda
Nobody is listening
They can hear the chants outside.
The country's stopped.

November twenty-seven, Noon
In Brno Students N through Y
Along with their Professor Z
Call "Strike."
Classrooms all are silent
Outside it is loud.
Classrooms all are empty
Outside is a crowd
"Free men do not live in fear"
We say while jingling our keys
"Communists subvert republic,
Havel to the castle now!"

IV

Found Text 4 (The Collapse)

SHIRLEY TEMPLE BLACK

Euphoric TV commentators carried live coverage of the nationwide, two-hour strike. The coverage began with scenes of television workers walking off their jobs. TV showed mass demonstrations in cities from Košice in Eastern Slovakia to Plzen in the western Czech Lands. This strike strengthens the Civic Forum's hand as it moves into an important round [of negotiations on Tuesday.

CIVIC FORUM

We demand changes of substance. If the prime minister's answer is positive, we shall negotiate with him and persist with our demands. If he does not accept this, we shall demand the resignation [of the government.

MARTIN 2

With the Communist Party on the run, millions of Czechoslovak students received the best news of their academic careers. The government said it planned to remove the constitutional provision that education be in the spirit of Marxism.

STUDENT 2

I prefer cherry lipstick to dialectical materialism. It's absolutely useless, an absolute bore, an absolute waste of time.

EMBASSY AID

Liberal Soviet lawmakers, watching the popular demand for political and economic reforms swell in Czechoslovakia, said here Monday that the time has come for Moscow to declare that the Warsaw Pact's suppression of the 1968 "Prague Spring" was wrong [and a setback for socialism.

COMMUNIST

Soviet leadership at that time supported the stand of one side in an internal dispute regarding objective pressing tasks. We share the view that the bringing in of armies in 1968 was unfounded, and that decision, in light of presently known facts, [was erroneous.

CIVIC FORUM

These are the demands of the Public Against Violence. We demand free elections as the basis for the transformation of the Slovak National Council into a real parliament of the Slovak nation. We demand freedom of enterprise, of assembly, of association, movement, conscience, and other civil rights and liberties.

STUDENT 3

The measures taken so far are not enough. The resignations are not enough. We will not rest until every member of the current government has resigned!

ALL (BUT COMMUNIST)

We are with you!

EMBASSY AIDE

It seemed somehow appropriate that when the old regime in Czechoslovakia formally agreed to cede its monopoly on power, the deed was done between a caretaker Prime Minister and an opposition lacking even a formal headquarters. So dizzyingly swift was the downfall of President Jakeš and his associates in the Communist leadership that when Prime Minister Adamec met today with Václav Havel and the Civic Forum, the participants seemed to be sweeping away some unpleasant remnants before plunging into the next and far more complex phase in the shaping of a post-Communist Czechoslovakia.

STUDENT 1

Our professor told us recently that our country was turning into a memorial display of Communism. But now we have taken our own way.

MARTIN 1

On Sunday, people surged into Wenceslas Square to hear Václav Havel and other dissidents speak once more. The crowd amounted in size to nearly a third of Prague's population.

EMBASSY AIDE

Residents of Prague, a city not famous for the sweetness of its manners, could not stop talking about how polite people were being to each other. Havel ended his speech by announcing "Truth and love will triumph over lies and hatred."

CIVIC FORUM, STUDENTS AND MARTINS

Truth and love will triumph over lies and hatred!

SHIRLEY TEMPLE BLACK

I invited a number of Civic Forum contacts to dinner at the residence. The dinner turned into something of a victory celebration. The mood was high, but not euphoric. The group appreciated that the Forum had a long road ahead of it. Their thoughts were now fixed on the possibility of Havel's election to the presidency.

SCENE 4 (AUDIENCE, PART 2)

(The OFFICER is at a table, drinking beer. VANĚK enters.)

OFFICER

Ferdinand!

VANĚK

What do you want?

OFFICER

Ferdinand, it's good to see you!

VANĚK

Are you bringing someone into custody? Who are you looking for?

OFFICER

We're not arresting anyone now. Not even the criminals.

VANĚK

Then what do you want?

OFFICER

Don't you remember me?

VANĚK

Yes, of course I remember you.

OFFICER

How are the hemorrhoids?

VANĚK

The hemorrhoids?

OFFICER

You have that problem, right? Like my uncle.

VANĚK

They're fine. They're not bothering me.

OFFICER

Good, so you see.

VANĚK

What?

OFFICER

I told you they would get better.

(Pause.)

VANĚK

Well, I should be going—

OFFICER

Listen, Ferdinand.

VANĚK

What is it?

OFFICER

I wanted to talk to you.

VANĚK

What about?

OFFICER

Sit down, won't you? I'll buy you a beer.

VANĚK

I'm not so fond of beer.

OFFICER

Everybody likes beer, right?

VANĚK

You don't need to buy me a beer.

OFFICER

Then have mine. I'll get myself a new one.

VANĚK

No, thank you.

(Pause.)

OFFICER

Listen, Ferdinand.

VANĚK

What is it?

OFFICER

I wanted to talk to you.

VANĚK

What about?

OFFICER

You know that fellow Havel, right?

VANĚK

I know him, yes.

OFFICER

Do you think he would join us?

VANĚK

Where?

OFFICER

Here. For a beer.

VANĚK

I think he's very busy right now.

OFFICER

Just tell him, there's this fellow I know, wants to meet you.

VANĚK

Really, there's so much going on—

OFFICER

You're friends, right?

VANĚK

Yes, we're friends.

OFFICER

So you can ask him.

VANĚK

I don't think now—

OFFICER

I see, I see, still going to hold it against me.

VANĚK

What?

OFFICER

It wasn't my fault you know. I was just doing a job. They told me what to do, and I did it. I was always on your side.

VANĚK

Were you?

OFFICER

I always treated you well, right? Didn't do anything too hard on you, did I?

VANĚK

You kept me in prison.

OFFICER

Well I had to do that, didn't I? That was my job. But I told you, I said, I hope that march of yours turns out well.

VANĚK

I don't remember your saying that.

OFFICER

Sure I did.

VANĚK
I don't remember it.

(Pause.)

OFFICER
Well, if I didn't say it, I certainly thought it.

VANĚK
I see.

OFFICER
You have to learn to read between the lines.

VANĚK
I see.

OFFICER
I was telling you by not telling you, if you know what I mean.

VANĚK
I don't.

OFFICER
I couldn't out and out tell you. So I deliberately didn't tell you I wanted the march to turn out well. Which should have told you that I did.

VANĚK
I should have guessed because you didn't say you wanted the march to turn out well that you wanted the march to turn out well?

OFFICER

Exactly.

VANĚK

How was I to guess that?

OFFICER

You're a writer, aren't you?

VANĚK

Yes, but that doesn't—

OFFICER

So you see.

(Pause.)

Listen, Ferdinand.

VANĚK

Yes?

OFFICER

When do you think you could get Havel to come here and join us for a beer?

VANĚK

Really I don't think—

OFFICER

He's your friend, right?

VANĚK

Yes.

OFFICER

So ask him then. Tell him, there's this guy who's been on our side all along, been one of our biggest supporters, just wants to thank you.

VANĚK

I'll pass the message on.

OFFICER

Then he'll come?

VANĚK

He's very busy—

OFFICER

But you're his friend, right?

VANĚK

Yes, but that doesn't mean—

OFFICER

Listen, Ferdinand. Maybe I can talk.

VANĚK

What do you mean?

OFFICER

In the square. In Wenceslas Square. With everyone else.

VANĚK

You want to talk in Wenceslas Square?

OFFICER

Sure. I'll say, listen, I may have been a member of the police, but I was working for you all along. From the inside. I didn't say anything, so they couldn't tell. But I was working for you.

VANĚK

What were you doing, exactly?

OFFICER

Like with you. Like what I did with you.

VANĚK

What did you do with me?

OFFICER

I told you I hoped the march would turn out well.

VANĚK

But you didn't tell me that.

OFFICER

You're a writer, aren't you? You have to read between the lines.

VANĚK

I see.

OFFICER

It was easy for you, Ferdinand. Much easier for you than it was for me.

VANĚK

How was it easier for me?

OFFICER
When you didn't believe in something, you could say you didn't believe in it. But me? What was I supposed to do?

VANĚK
You could have done the same.

OFFICER
Then who would there have been to help you, the way I helped you. Believe me, there wouldn't have been anyone else who would have bent over backwards the way I did. And if I had said something, believe me, there wouldn't have been anyone who would have been there for me. Would you have been there?

VANĚK
I would have supported you. The reason I was in jail was because I had signed a petition—

OFFICER
Your petition? Do you think anyone cared about your petition? They wanted me to find out about that march of yours. Not that you were much help there.

VANĚK
Are you angry I didn't tell you more?

OFFICER
You could have helped me out. Since you knew I was on your side.

VANĚK

You didn't say you were on my side.

OFFICER

That's how you should have known.

(Pause.)

Listen, Ferdinand...could you please tell Havel what I said?

VANĚK

I will

OFFICER

And he'll come?

VANĚK

I'll ask him.

OFFICER

Tell him, I want to speak in the Square.

VANĚK

I will

OFFICER

Tell him I was always on your side.

(Pause.)

You're not going to tell him. You're not going to tell him any of it.

VANĚK

Why do you say that?

OFFICER

I can read between the lines.

Chorus 4 (The Speeches)

CHORUS

December 3
"We must assess what's happened."
"Peaceful social change."
Free elections by July."

SOPRANO

What will happen?
What will happen now?
What will happen to me?
To my children?
My husband?
Better or worse?
I didn't like it before.
Will this be worse?
Do they know what they're saying?
Do they know what they're doing?

TENOR

I knew it.
When I was marching, then I knew it.
My parents said don't go, I went.
We all went.
They didn't know, too old to know,
Too old to hope like us.
I changed things.
When I marched that day I changed things.
Me. And all my friends.
We changed things

BARITONE

The way it was.
Back in '68.
Twenty years ago, or so.

Will it be like that again?
Times have changed.
For the better?
Could it be the same?

CHORUS

December 10
"The Communist Leader has resigned."
"Truth and love must prevail over lies and hatred!"

TENOR

They're gone
I can't believe they're gone.
Going. Gone.
I never thought that they would go.
They're as good as gone, now.
Good. Gone.
My father said they'd never go.
I said they'd go, they'd never go, they'd go.
They're gone.
All his life. All my life too.
And now it's changed. Over.
We've won.
I suppose we've won.
We're winning.
Won. It's done. We've won.

Truth and love.

CHORUS

December 17
"Czechoslovakia needs a president."
"I will accept it."

SOPRANO

I knew it
That's what he wanted
he says he didn't want it
But he wants it
Why accept it if he doesn't want it
What will happen now?
What will happen to me?
I didn't like it before.
Will this be worse?
Does he know what he is saying?
Does he know what he is doing?

TENOR

He'll win
There's no question that he'll win
No question
Everyone loves him
All these years
In the jail
All the protests
I can't believe he's winning
Can't believe he's won
Already won

My mother "impossible."
I thought she might be right
She wasn't
It's possible

SOPRANO

The way it was.
Will it be like Dubček back in '68
Twenty years ago, or so.
Times have changed.
Changing for the better.
Could it be the same?

CHORUS

January 1
People, your government has returned to you!

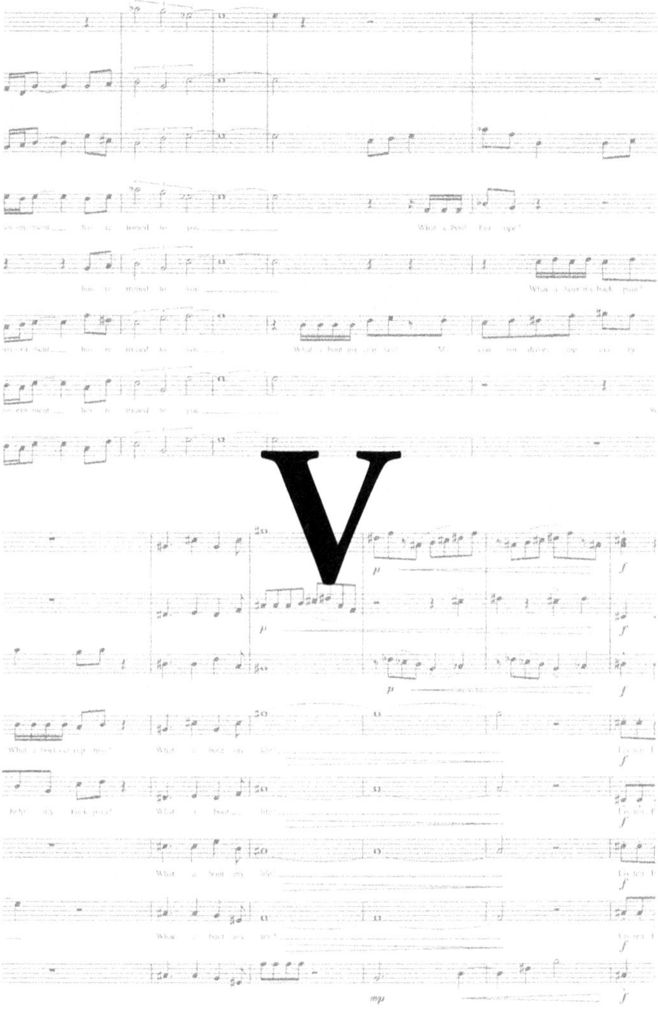

V

Found Text 5 (Havel President)

SHIRLEY TEMPLE BLACK

Telegram. Prague, the U. S Embassy. Shirley Temple Black, Ambassador. Václav Havel's interim election caps the first phase of the Czechoslovak "quiet" revolution. There is another election to come, in summer or fall of 1990, and the role that the Civic Forum and Havel will play in that election is unclear. Havel himself continues to dispute that his political position is anything but temporary. He has promised to resign after the next election. His eventual aim, he says, is to return to writing and theater. But we suspect he may find the presidency hard to leave. In any event, with Havel as President, the Civic Forum can now concentrate on the revolution's second stage: defining their democracy.

EMBASSY AIDE

The Velvet Revolution is coming to a close. The next steps will come harder.

SCENE 5 (UNVEILING)

(VANĚK is sitting with VERA and MICHAEL after dinner.)

VANĚK

That was wonderful. Thank you.

VERA

We're so glad you liked it.

MICHAEL

We're so glad you could come.

VERA

What with your new duties.

MICHAEL

But I told Vera, he must get lonely. Everyone wants some home-cooked food, a little wine...

VERA

Time with old friends.

MICHAEL

When times were bad, we always made sure you got some nice meals, so when times are good...

VERA

Why not continue the tradition?

VANĚK

Yes, of course. I've very much appreciated it.

(Pause.)

VERA
We saw Havel's speech

VANĚK
Did you?

VERA
Everyone did.

MICHAEL
Very inspiring.

VERA
Of course, no one can live up to the sort of expectations...

MICHAEL
But very inspiring, nonetheless.

VERA
So what's it like, to be part of the new government?

VANĚK
Well, we're still finding our feet really.

VERA
Yes, of course.

MICHAEL
That's only to be expected.

VERA

So many changes in such a short time. You must feel giddy.

MICHAEL

I know I do. Who would have thought?

VERA

Just a few years ago.

MICHAEL

A few months.

VERA

Yes, exactly, who would have thought?

MICHAEL

You in government, and us...

VANĚK

You're doing very well. You're still doing very well.

VERA

Yes. But not as good as you!

MICHAEL

Congratulations!

(Pause.)

Vera was cooking all day.

VANĚK

Really?

MICHAEL

But she saved the best for last.

VERA

Michael, you'll raise his expectations too much.

MICHAEL

Groobles.

VANĚK

What?

MICHAEL

Groobles. They're delicious. She learned the recipe in Switzerland.

VANĚK

Ah.

VERA

It's just something small. I know you can't stay much longer.

MICHAEL

Do you want some?

VANĚK

Certainly.

VERA

I'll get it.

(VERA exits.)

MICHAEL

I've heard things haven't been so easy.

VANĚK

Actually, I've been surprised at how well things have been going, considering.

MICHAEL

It must be hard for you, dealing with these international matters. You haven't been out of the country for over twenty years have you?

VANĚK

I wasn't allowed.

MICHAEL

Exactly. We had a hard time travelling ourselves, sometimes, because we were the known friends of so many dissidents. And now you all have to deal with international politics! No wonder you're having some difficulties.

VANĚK

Really, things have been going—

MICHAEL

You don't have to tell me. I understand.

(VERA enters with groobles.)

VERA

Here we are!

VANĚK

What are these again?

VERA

Groobles!

MICHAEL

She learned the recipe in Switzerland.

VANĚK

Ah.

(He tastes them,
experimentally.)

VERA

What do you think?

VANĚK

Mmmm.

MICHAEL

Right?

VERA

Hush.

MICHAEL

Vera makes the best groobles.

VERA

Michael.

MICHAEL

She does.

VANĚK

I'm sure.

(Pause.)

VERA

I forgot the wine.

VANĚK

No need.

MICHAEL

No, you must try it. It's wonderful dessert wine.

VERA

We bought it while we were in the Loire Valley.

MICHAEL

In France.

VERA

I'll get it.

(VERA exits.)

MICHAEL

I was hoping he would be a bit more astute on the domestic front, but then again, when you spend years in prison, you get a bit out of touch with everything, don't you?

VANĚK

You're talking about Havel?

MICHAEL

A bit frustrating to have him in charge sometimes, isn't it?

VANĚK

Not for me, really.

MICHAEL

You don't have to say anything. I understand.

(VERA enters with a tray and three glasses of wine.)

VERA

Here we are!

MICHAEL

Wonderful.

VERA

Try some.

VANĚK

Just a sip.

MICHAEL

To our new government!

(All three drink.)

A bit corked, don't you think Vera?

VANĚK

It seems very good.

MICHAEL

No, it's corked, I can tell.

VERA

You always have the best palette. They even told him so in France.

MICHAEL

We have that ice wine from Germany, don't we dear?

VERA

I'll get it.

VANĚK

No need.

VERA

Nonsense.

(VERA collects the glasses and exits with them.)

MICHAEL

You can tell us, Ferdinand.

VANĚK

Tell you what?

MICHAEL

Whatever you like. Whatever there is to tell.

VANĚK
There's nothing much to tell, really. Nothing you haven't already heard on the news.

MICHAEL
All right, I understand.

(Pause. VERA enters.)

VERA
I couldn't open the bottle.

MICHAEL
What?

VERA
The cork is stuck. It won't come out.

MICHAEL
You just have to pull on the corkscrew.

VERA
This one won't come out.

MICHAEL
Let me see. One moment, Ferdinand.

(MICHAEL exits.)

VERA
Grooble?

VANĚK
Oh. Yes. Thanks.

VERA
I learned the recipe in Switzerland.

VANĚK
Mmmmm.

(He chews it experimentally. She watches.)

VERA
We feel so terribly for you, Ferdinand.

VANĚK
Terribly? For me?

VERA
We know it's a lot to deal with.

VANĚK
Really, it's not so bad.

VERA
You can confide in us.

(MICHAEL enters, with bottle and corkscrew)

VANĚK
It's sort of fun, really.

MICHAEL
You're right. The cork is stuck.

VERA

See?

MICHAEL

I didn't think it could happen. But you're right. Ferdinard, hold onto the bottle.

(VANĚK takes the bottle. MICHAEL pulls, first straight, then under his legs.)

VERA

We want you to feel like you can tell us anything, Ferdinand.

MICHAEL

Still won't come. Vera, help me.

(VERA grabs onto MICHAEL and they pull together, contorting themselves.)

Vera's right, you should feel comfortable saying anything to us.

VANĚK

There's nothing really to tell.

MICHAEL

We understand.

VERA

We can read between the lines—

(VANĚK releases the bottle. VERA and MICHAEL fall over in a heap.)

VANĚK

I'm sorry. I couldn't hold on.

VERA

I'm afraid we can't open it.

MICHAEL

But Ferdinand was looking forward to it.

VANĚK

I'm fine without it.

VERA

Ferdinand was just about to tell us something.

MICHAEL

Was he?

VERA

Yes, he was.

MICHAEL

What were you going to tell us?

(Pause.)

VANĚK

I should go.

VERA

So soon?

VANĚK

My new duties...

VERA

But we have groobles.

MICHAEL

I'll work on that wine.

VANĚK

No need, really. I'm not that big a drinker.

VERA

I have other food, too.

MICHAEL

It's an evening of international cuisine.

VANĚK

I wish I could stay.

MICHAEL

I have some liquor.

VERA

Oh, he'd like the Chinese one. Made from pomegranate.

VANĚK

Thank you, no.

MICHAEL

So that's it then. Now you're so high and mighty.

VERA

Can't be bothered to even sit and have a drink with us.

MICHAEL

Too important for us now.

VERA

Don't have time for old friends anymore.

MICHAEL

No wonder everything's going so poorly.

VERA

I used to have pity for you. Now I think you just brought it on yourselves.

MICHAEL

No wonder the economy is failing.

VERA

No wonder there are criminals all over the streets.

MICHAEL

No wonder the country is going to split in half.

VERA

No wonder the rivers are flooding.

MICHAEL

It's all you selfish, selfish people. Won't even take the time to sit with us and eat groobles.

VERA

Aren't you ashamed?

(Pause.)

VANĚK

Maybe a taste of that liquor.

(Pause. Suddenly, VERA and MICHAEL are all smiles.)

MICHAEL

I'll have it for you in just one moment. Vera, will you put on some music?

VERA

Of course. Here Ferdinand, have another grooble.

Chorus 5 (Hubbub)

(The full cast enters.)

CHORUS

Your government has returned to you.

THE VOICE OF VÁCLAV HAVEL

I have a word of my own for this kind of phantasmagoric or dreamlike confusion of lines or variations of lines, and some minor nonsense, taken more or less at random from previous scenes. I call it a "hubbub," and I like to put it somewhere before the end, perhaps in the place where catharsis is supposed to occur. What is it? A prelude to some final raveling or unraveling of the plot? A metaphor for the chaos of the world or the chaos in the mind of the main character? A pure expression of authorial mischief? A product of dramatic logic? A deliberate trick? Probably all three of the above.

OFFICER

Listen…

STANĚK

Listen…

VERA

Listen…

MICHAEL

Listen…

MARTINS
Listen, Ferdinand!

OFFICER
You're a peaceful sort of fellow

STANĚK
To seeing each other again!

VERA
Time with old friends!

MICHAEL
When times are good...

MARTIN 1
I'm Martin.

MARTIN 2
And he's also Martin!

VERA AND MICHAEL
Listen, Ferdinand.

OFFICER
You're friends with him, right?

STANĚK
Havel.

MARTINS 1 & 2
And that lot.

MICHAEL
You don't have to tell us, we understand.

VERA AND OFFICER
We can read between the lines.

VERA, MICHAEL, MARTINS, AND OFFICER
Listen, Ferdinand.

SHIRLEY TEMPLE BLACK
Telegram. Prague, the U. S Embassy.

STUDENT 1
Clamor in the East.

STUDENT 2
I prefer cherry lipstick.

COMMUNIST
Socialist renewal.

CIVIC FORUM
There is no West Czechoslovakia, but if there were, I'd be the first to go.

EMBASSY AIDE
The next steps will come harder.

ALL BUT VANĚK
Listen, Ferdinand!

CHORUS

Listen, Ferdinard...
You're the only one that I can tell
I'm not so sure about what happens next
You were in the revolution
You are in the government
You're Havel's friend, so you can tell us
What are the plans?
What about the crime?
What about pollution?
What about our money?
What about our schools?
What about the Slovaks, can we remain united?
Do we punish all the Communists?
What about these taxes?
What about the heating in my house, it's not
working in my house
What about the unemployment?
What about the army?
Where are all the companies and their investments?
What about the theater?
What about my pension?
You government has returned to you.
What about Europe?
What about my cousin, my cousin drives me crazy
What about my back pain, can someone help my
back pain?
What about the mafia?
What about corruption?
What about my life?

Listen, Ferdinand...
Mission accomplished,

Revolution won
I'm sure we'll disagree sometimes.
Listen Ferdinand…
But you're a clever fellow,
You'll figure all this out,
You seem to know a lot,
Things are going well, very well so far,
Listen Ferdinand…
But can you tell us
Why don't you tell us?
Tell us
Tell us
Tell us
What's next?

Have to do the laundry
Have to visit Mom and Dad for dinner
Have to get the shower fixed
Have to get a haircut
Have to buy some clothes
Have to clean the house.
Have to fix the car.
Have to go to school
Have to pay the bills
Have to reap reports.
Have to go to work.
Have to, have to, have to, have to

Did you see the—
Did you read the—
Did you see or read the papers…

The prime minister is on the…

Have to pick up groceries for tonight
Have to have the dentist check my teeth.
Have to make sure that the baby eats.
Have to start my diet soon.
Have other things to do.

I'm going home
Am I late?
My boyfriend and I have plans
Tomorrow
A movie
We have plans.

APPENDIX
Velvet Revolution Timeline

November 9
The Berlin Wall falls.

November 17
A peaceful student demonstration commemorating Jan Opletal, a Czech protestor killed by the Nazis, evolves into an anti-Communist march. It is violently disrupted by the police. That evening, students and members of the theater community agree to go on strike.

November 18
Rumors fly that a young student, Martin Šmid, was killed during the march. Theaters open their stages for public political discussions.

November 19
It is discovered that the rumors of Šmid's death are false. Václav Havel and other Charter 77 signatories in Prague form the Civic Forum. In Bratislava, they form the Slovak Public Against Violence.

November 21
Prime Minister Adamec meets with the Civic Forum, though he refuses entrance to Havel.

November 22
Havel addresses a crowd of 20,000 from a balcony over Wencelas Square and called for a general, nationwide strike. The Civic Forum chooses a theater called Laterna Magika as its headquarters.

APPENDIX
Velvet Revolution Timeline
(continued)

November 24
Miloš Jakeš, head of the Communist party, resigns. The more moderate Karel Urbánek takes his place.

November 26
Prime Minister Adamec appears with Havel and former Czech leader Alexander Dubček in front of an audience of one million at Letna Plain. Adamec is booed and hissed, until he is forced to retreat.

November 27
A successful general strike is held across the country.

November 29
The General Assembly deletes the constitutional provision referring to a leading role of the Communist party, effectively ending Communist rule.

December 10
President Husák resigns. Elections are planned, and Havel reluctantly agrees to run.

December 29
Havel is elected president.

January 1
Havel's first address as president. He ends it by declaring "Your government has returned to you."

www.ingramcontent.com/pod-product-compliance
Lightning Source LLC
LaVergne TN
LVHW021509080426
835509LV00018B/2458
9780977019731